ALBERTA FERRETTI

ALBERTA FERRETTI

Edited by Samuele Mazza
and Giusi Ferré

Gingko
PRESS

On the cover
March 1997, (photo by Fabio Pettinari)

Translation: Christopher Evans

First published in Italy
©1998 by Leonardo Arte s.r.l., Milan, Elemond Editori Associati

Published in the United States of America by Gingko Press Inc.
5768 Paradise Drive, Suite J - Corte Madera, CA 94925
Tel: (415) 924-9615 - Fax: (415) 924-9608 email: gingko@linex.com

ISBN 3-927258-59-8

Printed in Italy

Luxury, calm and lightness

To express her own creativity, Alberta Ferretti has adopted an approach typical of the artist, that is the tactile and visual recognizability of her work. Her creativity stems from a profound understanding of femininity, just as her awareness of taste is based on a recurrent theme. This is why her collections, though made up of hundreds of models, always have a leitmotiv that is renewed in a surprising manner from season to season. It is the slip that represents a sort of ensemble of veils without season. Or rather, that is able to represent all four seasons, as an almost timeless, eternal garment. Veils that conjure up the atmosphere of the Renaissance, the elegance conveyed by the three Graces in Botticelli's *Allegory of Spring*, evoking centuries of innocent pictorial sensuality created out of fabrics that are embroidered, printed or overlaid in different shades of color. An alchemy of fabrics-non-fabrics, always precious, impalpable and light, used to create clothing suited to women who are at once ethereal and flirtatious, women who like to seduce without the aid of trinkets, through an extreme simplicity of gestures and accessories.

The principal characteristic of Alberta Ferretti's style lies in the pureness of essence. Perhaps this is why her clothes, however eye-catching, do not impose themselves on the personality of the wearer. This is a characteristic that can also be discerned in Philosophy, the line that Ferretti has conceived for women with a preference for a style whose contemporaneity lies somewhere between the dynamism of the big city and personal appeal.

In the world of "Made in Italy," Alberta Ferretti is considered not just one of the rising stars of creative design but also, in her role at the head of AEFFE, alongside her brother Massimo Ferretti, the proprietor of one of the most important Italian companies in the luxury market, now seen as a university of international style. It is here, in fact, that the collections of Jean-Paul Gaultier, Rifat Ozbek, Moschino and Narciso Rodriguez are produced and distributed. Four names that represent four different currents in contemporary fashion, brought together by a company that is able to offer them a tried-and-tested experience of production.   *samuele mazza*

Alberta Ferretti has brought to her work the same grace with which, as a child, she played in her mother's workshop. Games played with fabric, knotting, cutting and sewing, amidst the scent of new silk and the inviting rustle of taffetta. Quiet games, in which she thought that the greatest fun was to be had from inventing dresses and pinning hems, checking with the forewoman if the skirt fell right, the turn of the collar was impeccable, the waist neither too loose nor too tight. And now that she designs four collections a year, she is applauded and sought-after by the most elegant actresses, as well as by music and TV stars. She is admired and interviewed and has shows in Milan and Los Angeles. This minute and tireless woman has not lost that joy and enthusiasm that makes her unique. That light touch that makes her style so different and her way of presenting herself so delicate, through the places in which she works, shows her dresses and lives. "Il faut être léger comme l'oiseau et non comme la plume," wrote Paul Valéry. It is to this lightness, which reminds us that human beings are made of the same substance as dreams, that the book is dedicated. Rather than a history of facts, a tale of emotions. For those who know that all we need is to dress ourselves with symbols, metaphors, allegories, the wind.

milano, palazzo donizetti in a sketch by kris ruhs

the world of alberta ferretti

backstage helmut newton

A collection, for Alberta Ferretti, is only finished when the show is over. Up to the last moment she adjusts, alters and intervenes, paring away in search of that ideal atmosphere that ought to be created between a woman and her clothes. Even when she is choosing the fabrics and designs, she is looking for this ideal harmony, seduced by the memory of a painting, inspired by a book or a film. "I don't have just one muse, but many," says the designer. "I'm inspired by milieus—France and England of the thirties, the Berlin of the twenties— rather than by an individual presence. I follow my feelings—silver, metal, the future, as for the summer of '98—rather than sticking rigidly to a plan." Like pieces of a mosaic, her collections often feature women travelers, the eccentric English countesses portrayed by Cecil Beaton, the tender deities of Alma Tadema: everything that she loves and translates into her dresses, following the promptings of a personal taste that has been refined by time. "I have discovered that it is meticulous care over trimmings that determines change." Perhaps Aby Warburg, as a good art historian, was exaggerating when he said "God is hidden in the details," but what a profound observation it is.

alberta ferretti backstage, photographed by scianna

Slip. Like a mild obsession, this dress-cum-undergarment recurs in all Alberta Ferretti's collections. Slips of chiffon, georgette, organza, one on top of the other, even of wool and masculine heathered melange cloth to underline the contrast between the softness of forms and the terseness of the fabric. The first of these that the designer created to her full satisfaction (early eighties), and still has clearly in her mind, was the one made of pearl gray satin, bias-cut and as liquid on the body as water. With wide or very thin straps, in the Empire style or straight, the combination is the strongest mark of a delicate style. "Perhaps for its forms, perhaps because it alludes to the secrets of intimacy, I consider it the most feminine garment there is," comments Alberta Ferretti. "The one that I never tire of designing because it lends itself to infinite variations." Regarding naturalness as one of the qualities of feminine elegance, she appreciates it when part of the slip shows under the jacket or cardigan, "which makes it less provocative and more sensual." Hinting at what's underneath, with its hand-stitched hems or chiffon borders barely visible on the satin, or with minute hem-stitches instead of broad and rigid edgings, the garment is as light as a breath of wind.

spring summer 97 – chiffon and embroidered border

spring summer 97 – beads and double chiffon
opposite: fall winter 97/98 – embroidery on organza

fall winter 97/98 – embroidery on double chiffon

spring summer 97 – bead trimmings

fall winter 97/98 – velvet borders
opposite: fall winter 97/98 – a garden of embroidery

Flowers. Glimpsed through the transparent material, the tangled branches of wisteria winding round trees. The stylized pattern of hydrangea bushes outlined in beads that shine like dew. Fantastic petals embroidered on blue silk, their vaguely abstract nature recalling branches of coral. There is a strong scent of flowers in Alberta Ferretti's world. A woman who lives among flowers, who loves and takes care of them personally "everyday because that is the only way to make the house feel alive, as if it were animated by a constant presence." The designer likes to draw and work in the open air, in the peace and quiet of her sheltered garden as soon as the weather permits. When the jasmine climbs the walls without effort, all mixed up with the Virginia creeper, and the hydrangeas are forming large clumps of color in the flowerbeds. A constant source of inspiration, when they are transferred onto fabric, Alberta Ferretti's flowers grow blurred, suggesting an intensity of color, the shadow of a tonality. They turn into stylized drawings that are only just discernible. Sometimes attenuated and veiled by a layer of chiffon. Other times re-elaborated by patterns and prints. Essence and illusion, rather than well-defined image.

fall winter 92/93 – thread and beads on peau–d'ange satin

spring summer 97 - all-over embroidery

autumn winter 92/93 – china land
opposite: autumn winter 97/98 – devoré

spring summer 92 – petals made of silk organza

Precious. There is a sort of modesty, almost a reserve in the elegance of the embroideries and jais, velvets and silks, proposed by Alberta Ferretti. The closer you look, the more you become aware of a luxurious and discreet splendor, expressed by a thousand details: beads that are tiny and never too shiny, that may just trace a line or cover the whole garment, transforming the knitwear into a kind of jewelry. Along with honeycomb velvet, embroidery on shoes (a tradition, ever since 1988), heathered melange and stretch flannel mixed with chiffon and iridescent organza. It is the simplicity of certain materials, combined with the gracious richness of others, that creates the contrast which represents true modernity today. To suggest a different sense of what is precious while maintaining a pure and essential line. Alberta Ferretti works on contrasts, uniting masculine and feminine materials, fabrics that would appear to be reserved for the daytime and those usually dedicated to the evening. In her collection for the summer of 1998, this revolution in luxury has been extended to the unfinished hem, to lace applied by hand and frayed, to the carefully-gauged tear. Aesthetic heresies that seem to belong to the great current of Arte Povera.

fall winter 97/98 - macramé knitwear embroidered with beads

fall winter 97/98 – paolo roversi for alberta ferretti

alberta ferretti boutique – small chairs in fortuny fabric and gided metal

Lightness. An approach to life, a canon of taste, a necessity. Lightness is at once the dream and the reality of Alberta Ferretti, to whom we can apply the description that Italo Calvino (in his *Lezioni Americane*) made of his own work. "What I have been doing most of the time is to remove weight." In her quest for this lightness, Alberta Ferretti has made the difficult choice of eliminating and discarding, of purifying her clothes: ever thinner shoulder-straps and more impalpable fabrics, the structure more and more essential. Reduced (in the 1998 summer collection) to a thread of nylon concealed in the edging to support the more fluid necklines. If the feminine image of her garments has the force of a vision, their settings also reflect this unmistakable taste. The headquarters in Milan, the historic Palazzo Donizetti, glows with a soft and diffuse glimmer, its stuccoes, plasterwork and moldings painted in cream and gold and the furnishings—white drapes, glass-topped tables, gilded metal chairs—apparently designed in the absence of gravity. Just by hints, just by light and shade. As in Alberta Ferretti's stores, with their sparse furniture designed by Kris Ruhs, their crystal chandeliers and broken mosaics.

spring summer 97 – on chiffon, inlays of chiffon

spring summer 97 – velvet sandals – by kind permission of vogue italia

fall winter 97/98 – embroidery and scalloped edging
opposite: spring summer 97 – pin tucks as designs

in the following pages: spring summer 98

Advertising. Alberta Ferretti's clothes cast a spell on photographers. In their search for the perfect image, the atmosphere is charged with innocence, the models are transfigured. Through Paolo Roversi's lens, Tanga, Lonneke and Jenny Knight (the protagonists of the 97/98 images) take on the enchanted lightness of Alma Tadema's child-goddesses. Shalom Harlow (Fall–Winter 94/95) seems to have escaped from A Midsummer Night's Dream. Amber Valletta (Fall–Winter 93/94) has the sort of pageboy-grace that would have fascinated Fernand Khnopff, the painter of Pre-Raphaelite ambiguity. In the eyes of these photographers, it is possible to catch a common gleam, the reflection of the charm worked by Alberta Ferretti's style on very different talents. From Fabrizio Ferri (Spring–Summer 90), who lost himself with Tatiana among the dunes of San Diego, California, to Steven Meisel, who relied on the bare purity of the studio. Ellen von Unwerth immersed the fragile women of the winter of '96 in New York traffic. But it is Paolo Roversi, whose path has twice crossed that of Alberta Ferretti, who manages to give the most complete expression to the designer's world, in an aesthetic journey toward perfection.

steven meisel spring summer 1997, spring summer 1996

steven meisel spring summer 1994   **ellen von unwerth fall winter 95/96**

steven meisel fall winter 94/95

steven meisel fall winter 91/92

steven meisel fall winter 93/94

steven meisel fall winter 90/91   spring summer 88

paolo roversi spring summer 86

Friends. There are friends she has always had, and there are chance meetings that turn into relationships of mutual esteem and liking. Andie MacDowell, who has known her for some time and is fascinated by her understanding of elegance, puts it like this: "Alberta Ferretti wins you over with her sweetness and attentiveness." There are many show-biz personalities who have got to know her and who often wear her clothes: Kate Winslet, the singers Sheryl Crow and Suzanne Vega. Some of her dresses hang in the wardrobes of Angelica Huston and Nicole Kidman. Andie MacDowell looked charming in her green macramé slip at the Academy Awards. But she has many other confidants and friends: from Helmut Newton to Steven Meisel, star photographers. From Franca Sozzani, editor of *Vogue Italia*, to the jewelry designer Marina Schiano. From Jean-Paul Gaultier to Professor Luc Montagnier, for whom she organized an important charity performance with the invaluable assistance of Zucchero Fornaciari, donating all the profits to research against AIDS. And in Los Angeles (June 97) she took part in the event staged by the Neiman Marcus department stores, engaged in other sectors of research. With discretion, she is always involved in Italian initiatives. As a friend.

andie macdowell

susanne bartsch–alberta ferretti

angelica huston

bob geldof–alberta ferretti

franca sozzani–marina schiano–alberta ferretti

luc montagnier–alberta ferretti

miriam makeba

jean-paul gaultier-alberta ferretti

madonna

marina schiano

alberta ferretti-kate winslet

zucchero-alberta ferretti

steven meisel–alberta ferretti

melanie griffith

helmut newton–alberta ferretti

to alberta from...

nicole kidman
How can Alberta Ferretti manage to propose a luxurious fashion that is, at the same time, fresh and light as if it were weightless? In one word, beautiful to behold and pleasant to wear.

hamish bowles - european editor-at-large american *vogue*
Alberta Ferretti is fashion's great romantic. Hers is the world of the great early twentieth century lingeries, of fine linens trellised with cut-work, of chiffon worked with spidery ladders of faggoting. But because she's a modern romantic, these ethereal creations are whipped up in state-of-the-art factories, they're cut by lasers and crafted with extraordinarily innovative machines, proving that beauty can be born out of high-tech innovation.

andie macdowell.
I met Alberta Ferretti on the eve of the Oscars when I visited her showroom in Milan: her sense of design surrounds you the minute you walk in the door. You feel her strong yet feminine touch. The collection held many beautiful things and trying on the designs under her watchful eye made me very secure. By her example and her design you never feel objectified in your beauty, and can embrace your femininity completely.

angelica blechschmidt - editor-in-chief german *vogue*
Fashion is a liveable dream, a fragile yet powerful reminder that there is more to dressing than serious suits. Alberta Ferretti is today's true, new romantic. In her sylph we meet the creature every woman secretly yearns to be.

natalia aspesi - correspondent *la repubblica*
Light and graceful, evanescent and volatile as if feminine
sensuality were weightless, and living in delicate silence,
Alberta Ferretti's fashion resembles her. It resembles this woman
with a child-like smile who is a gentle but tenacious entrepre-
neur, producing clothes with fun and love, who makes women
believe that it is their feminine gracefulness to render them
winners.

franca sozzani - editor-in-chief italian *vogue*
Little delicate sheaths peeking out of dresses to become unique
pieces. Extremely precious "ripped" chiffon that moves on and
with the body. Light, delicate, almost impalpable: an Alberta
Ferretti woman.

kris ruhs - artist
We worked together in creating her world: her warm friendship
makes everything a pleasure.

paola cacianti - rai tg1 television news reporter
Sensual, yet chaste slipdresses, non-provoking necklines,
transparencies to be discerned.
If I only had a word to define Alberta Ferretti's style it would be
moderation. The clever balance in a dress where creativity is
found in detail (an *à jour* embroidery instead of a seam; the
"unfinished" fabric orderly frayed) and lightness doesn't
compromise wearability.

At home. In the old villa where she lives, at San Giovanni in Marignano, Alberta Ferretti has preserved the vault ceilings, the floor with its large terracotta tiles and the fireplaces. To the original structure she has added the windows of the upper floor, which let in the honey yellow sunlight, a blend of the country and the seaside. "I need to feel the presence of tradition, history, around me," she says. "I like to look for connections between the past and the present." Before subjecting the villa to a thorough restoration, she waited to get a "feeling" for the house by living in it, changing only what was indispensable and hanging up the much-loved pictures that she has been collecting for years. When she felt ready, she set about restructuring and furnishing it by herself as the fancy took her. "I'm not attracted by the perfect coherence of a style. As the form interests me more than the period, I look for a logical and emotional thread that can link an art déco armchair with a footrest made out of an eighteenth-century Indian parasol." So the table of glass and stone is ringed by late 18th century ivory-colored lacquered chairs. Among the Biedermeier furniture hangs a picture by Julian Schnabel, while antique Indian chairs with their backs carved into the shape of fantastic animals await guests in the garden. san giovanni in marignano - entering the house

montegridolfo: at palazzo viviani...

Montegridolfo. It's the story of an "Ever Ever Land," restored to its original beauty and above all to its people. The story of a spell cast by a castle set on a hill, in the place where the border between the lands of the Malatesta, lords of Rimini, and those of the Montefeltro, who made Urbino great, used to run in the Renaissance. Palazzo Viviani was in bad shape, as were the houses around it. Decrepit and yet beautiful, enclosed by walls that seem to outline the slender form of a ship. Alberta Ferretti saw them and was enchanted. Together with a group of friends, the town of Montegridolfo—which is a tiny but real village still populated by its original inhabitants and various institutions, she has brought the place back to life. Now it is all stone and light, cobblestones and wooden shutters, flowers on the balconies and at the windows. "We have kept it as natural and humble as possible, using salvaged material," she explains. Palazzo Viviani has become the most hospitable of hotels. And often, as you walk through the streets, you can hear the pupils of Gustav Kuhn practicing their instruments and music, in the Musical Academy that the maestro has been able to found.

milan – the alberta ferretti boutique in a sketch by kris ruhs

ALBERTA FERRETTI

milan – the philosophy boutique

Settings. Boutiques that seem to have been decorated with light and air, with the warm glint of gold and starry silver. Old palaces transformed into showrooms: the spaces where Alberta Ferretti receives her customers express the same personality as her clothes. With that light touch of poetry, of quiet and seductive splendor. "But I always prefer to go beyond the perfection of a single style to add a touch of the unexpected." And Palazzo Donizetti in Milan is surprising: attributed to one of the most famous of Italian architects, Piero Portaluppi, it was built around 1920 in an eclectic style that blends the baroque with art nouveau and with such precious details as the late seventeenth-century coffered ceiling. A bizarre mixture of inspirations and references that has been maintained even in the furnishings: modern, with pieces designed by Kris Ruhs out of gilded metal and glass to accentuate the sense of lightness. The showroom on 56th Street in New York is even older: a building constructed in 1902 for the banker Seligman by C.P.H. Gilbert, a prestigious architectural studio specializing in the château and Gothic style. "Finding it was a mark of destiny," claims Alberta Ferretti. "It even has an oval hall and a ceiling similar to those of Palazzo Donizetti."

Philosophy. Like a younger sister who wanted to make her own way, Alberta Ferretti's line for young people changed its name as it went along. It has smoothed off its sharp corners and strengthened various aspects of its personality. When it was created in 1984 (the first line was already five years old), it was given an imposing and decidedly long name: Ferretti Jeansphilosophy. It was dedicated to young women with a passion for a casual, natural style, a certain impetuosity, an arrogant freshness. Taking a few seasons to find its feet, this collection set off in the direction of a universe of sparkling energy, quite independent of that of Alberta Ferretti. Surrounded by a world of music, live performers and crowds, she also won over Camilla, the energetic presenter of video-clips on MTV. Shows were organized that looked like jazz sessions, with rock bands and singers on the catwalk: from Heather Small to Suzanne Vega. The line became famous when it was worn by television personalities that everyone was talking about, like Ambra. It was only natural that one day it should decide to shorten its name. Now known simply as Philosophy, it made its debut in October 1995 (Spring–Summer 1996). While Ferretti's first line is reticent and discreet and chooses the almost atelier-like intimacy of Palazzo Donizetti to show itself off,

Philosophy likes company, invites all its friends and chooses locations for its shows that attract the creative, the denizens of the night, the disco-crazy. In the big industrial spaces of Milan, around the railroad and in abandoned factories, it has organized shows-cum-events-cum-parties with live concerts by the group Freak Power and over two thousand guests. Fascinated, like all the younger generation, by technology, computers, the mutant hybridization of video, bit, space and time, Philosophy held its parades one season surrounded by screens and allusions to the future, in a magical urban atmosphere. Even its clothes have undergone subtle mutations, feeling the influence of a continually evolving society: "Rather than to a woman," explains Alberta Ferretti, "Philosophy is dedicated to an idea: youth. Dedicated to the young in years, the young at heart, the young in taste." So by mixing influences and the fascination of encounters with other worlds, an urban collection was born that seemed to bring together different ethnic groups and worlds (Fall–Winter 97/98). While for Spring–Summer 98 there is in the delicate sheen of the fabrics, in the patterns that look like streaks of silver, in the metal wire that is interwoven with the fibers to provide both strength and light, a dream of the future. An encounter with the new millennium.

milan – the philosophy boutique in a sketch by kris ruhs

fall winter 97/98 – contrasts of wool and chiffon

fall winter 97/98 – appliqués of organza

fall winter 97/98 – the
surprise of different materials

spring summer 98 – glints of silver
and shiny brushstrokes

Advertising. Aristocratic little girls resembling overgrown Alices in Wonderland, young women with languid gestures who look like they stepped out of a Pre-Raphaelite painting: from the tender metropolitan warriors of the early campaigns who played with symbols and signs on T-shirts, Philosophy has come to the sophisticated image of today. Where youth has become a synonym for subtle intelligence, restrained passion, education. Portrayed by Paolo Roversi as girls from an English college, the models bring a breath of fresh air and eccentricity with their gazes and attitudes, even against the bare background of the studio. Mark Borthwick, the young photographer who had been responsible for the previous campaigns, chose instead to immerse the models in a rarefied atmosphere, treating the outdoor setting (a garden) as if it were an old studio backdrop. Images suspended in unreality that were also used for an unusual outdoor campaign: a mean often chosen for this line targeted at the younger generation, who are pictured as active consumers of city life. "The woman who wears the clothes of the Philosophy line lives in today's world without being overwhelmed by it," says Alberta Ferretti. "She has modern tastes but is aware of her roots in tradition."

paolo roversi fall winter 97/98

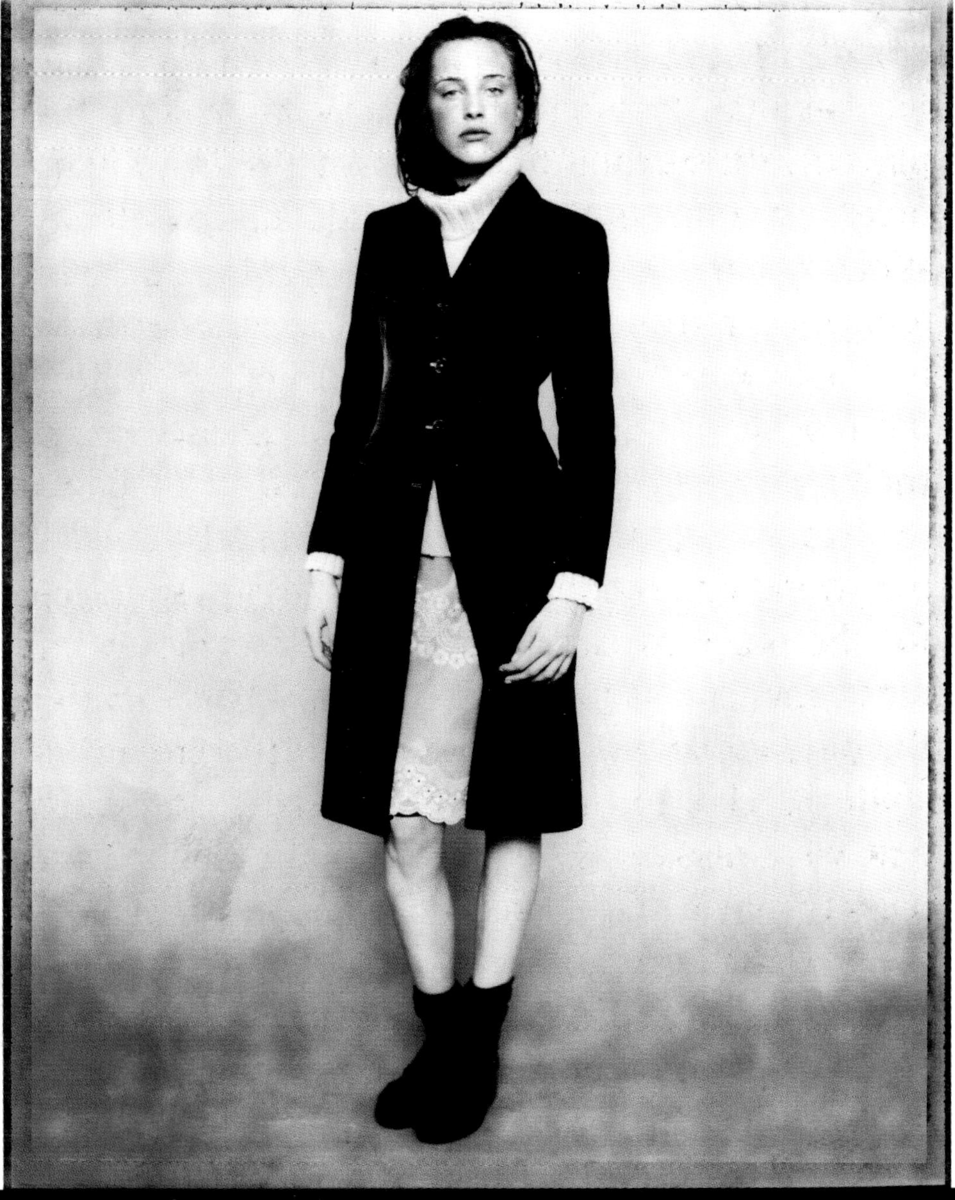

mark borthwick fall winter 96/97

simona cavallari

sheryl crow

suzanne vega

camila

heather small

stefania rocca–alberta ferretti–simona cavallari

amadeus–alessia marcuzzi

ambra

corona

memories are made of this

camila raznovich - mtv

I fell in love with Philosophy because it expresses all the femininity of young and modern women. I am attracted by its freshness and simplicity and I find that Philosophy, with its gentle, romantic yet strong dresses, complements perfectly my impetuous and "masculine" personality.

I like it because I feel it close to my world, the musical one; I like to wear Philosophy everyday, and I like its slight touch of rock 'n 'roll. I was lucky to collaborate with Alberta Ferretti and I was struck by her energy, her passion for her work and the great attention she pays to detail.

iain r. webb - fashion director *elle* uk

Ferretti's Philosophy line effortlessly bridges the gap between ancient and modern. They are wearable pleasures. Being a man I must admit a pang of jealousy when I see my female counterparts dressed in these beautiful clothes, although I would still like them to be mine: I would simply hang them on the wall and gaze at them.

patti o'brien - fashion director *rolling stone*

Alberta Ferretti is one of the most influential designers today. Her Philosophy collection is modern and sexy, with its sense of fluidity and femininity without being fussy, and the mix of velvet, suede and leather with touches of transparencies that work for day or evening.

heather small - m people

Philosophy di Alberta Ferretti clothes are timelessly elegant, like the lady herself.

alessia marcuzzi - tv star

My home is my wardrobe. And my wardrobe consists of a suitcase that moves with me, containing only the bare necessities: my fennel infusion, my music, two books, my mobile phone, my game-boy, my bran flakes, and my Philosophy clothes. Essential, simple and elegant clothes, that at first glance don't seem to add anything more to my personality, but, instead, they are my personality, because wearing Philosophy makes me feel at home.

philosophy – the future in the show

cuttings

corriere della sera (5-10-1997)
Le ragazzine di Philosophy, linea giovane di Alberta Ferretti, le puoi invece incontrare ogni giorno sull'autobus. Non portano tacchi alti, cattivi, ma sandali bassi. Hanno i capelli sciolti, il trucco invisibile. Delicate, vanno a scuola in primavera indossando gonne al ginocchio, con giacche di pelle a sacchetto o cappottini stretch. In estate hanno abiti in organza, uno sopra l'altro, dolci fantasie di fiori. Ma è il cangiante che domina la collezione: grigi, blu, rosa, beige hanno i bagliori del metallo. *paola pollo*

la repubblica (5-10-1997)
Paiono uscite da film muti in bianco e nero ("Metropolis", "Giglio infranto") queste malinconiche Lilian Gish, queste timide Brigitte Helm. Sui loro corpicini smunti, di fragile e irresistibile carnalità, gli abiti grigi hanno un lucore notturno, che è poi il pallore del corpo sotto garze argentate; le maglie quasi metalliche e tenui, hanno riflessi cangianti che predispongono al mistero. *natalia aspesi*

international herald tribune (11-3-1997)
There is also something quintessentially Italian in the delicate work on sheer fabrics shown by Alberta Ferretti. She captured famininity in exquisite apron-dresses, yet made lingerie-light fabrics work for modern life by putting them with cloud-soft cardigans or tailored gray coats with raised seaming. *suzy menkes*

le figaro (11-3-1997)
Alberta Ferretti est délicate comme une "lingère de fin" d'autrefois. Sous chaque jupe et chaque robe dépasse une chemise d'organza blanc festonnée comme un jupon de petite fille. *jamie samet*

the times (9-10-1996)
Alberta Ferretti: the prettiest clothes of all.
But there was still one show in Milan where everything—the frills, the lace, the see-through fabrics and pallid colour palette—fitted into place. Alberta Ferretti's main-line collection was the best example this season of how fashion can (and should) be directional and wearable, simultaneously. By adding a black slip and black opaque tights under her pretty nothing dresses, Ferretti didn't need the big knickers. *iain r. webb*

corriere della sera (7-10-1996)
Anche Alberta Ferretti, con i suoi romantici abiti leggiadri, aerei di chiffon e voile di cotone, dai tagli anatomici e dai ricami di cristallo, riesce a dare grazia ai corpi pur sottili delle modelle. Una collezione veramente indovinata.
laura dubini

chronology

1950

Alberta Ferretti was born in Gradara, under the sign of Taurus with Leo in the ascendant. In the dressmaker's workshop run by her mother she breathes the scent of fabric, plays with scissors and learns to cut and sew.

1968

She opens her first boutique in Cattolica, 5 miles from Riccione, on the Adriatic Riviera.

1968

At a very young age, she marries and soon has two sons: Giacomo and Simone. Her house has a boutique on the ground floor, an apartment on the second floor with the children and a workshop on the third with two assistants who make up skirts and blouses, the first clothes designed by Alberta Ferretti for her store.

1974

An agent, who has entered the store to show her the wonders of who knows what collection, is attracted by the clothes that he sees and asks "Whose are they?" And Ferretti answers: "Mine." That year she decides to prepare an entire collection: the first, under her name.

1980

At San Giovanni in Marignano she founds the company of which she is the Vice President and which she calls AEFFE, after the initials of her name. Over the years the company will sign a series of contracts for the production and distribution of the collections of famous designers (from 1980 to 1985 Enrico Coveri; 1983 Moschino; 1988 Rifat Ozbek; 1994 Jean-Paul Gaultier; 1997 Narciso Rodriguez).

1981

In October she shows her first collection in Milan, which is on its way to becoming the new capital of the fashion world.

1984
She creates Ferretti Jeansphilosophy, dedicated to the younger generation, which is then renamed Philosophy di Alberta Ferretti.

1994
On June 24, after a long and enthusiastic effort to bring the place back to life, Montegridolfo, a small village of medieval origin on the borders of Urbino and Montefeltro, reopens its gates. Alberta Ferretti and her brother Massimo, president of AEFFE, have made great efforts to renovate the village, restoring it to an unexpected splendor. They also made an important contribution to the foundation of the Musical Academy: a workshop of "cultured" music directed by Gustav Kuhn and intended for young artists interested in experimenting with different musical languages.

1994
Palazzo Donizetti, the showroom in Milan, is inaugurated: a building constructed in an eclectic style around 1920 and attributed to Piero Portaluppi, a prominent exponent of the Milanese "Novecento" style.

1996
Opening of the showroom in New York (56th Street) in a building designed by C.P.H. Gilbert in 1902 for the banker Henry Seligman. Completely restored in the European classical style which tones down even the most opulent details by the use of pale colors, it houses all the lines produced by AEFFE.

1997
March: the Alberta Ferretti collection is described as "the most beautiful of the season" (TG Uno).

1998
AEFFE in San Giovanni in Marignano covers an area of over 22,000 square meters, employs over 500 people, has 2500 clients all over the world and produces more than a million garments a year.

special thanks to:

GIUSI FERRÉ E CARLA FARÉ

who have constructed this book

UFFICIO STAMPA ALBERTA FERRETTI

BOX2 MILANO

STEFANO PECCATORI

MILES ALDRIDGE

MARIA VITTORIA BACKHAUS

SETTIMIO BENEDUSI

MARK BORTHWICK

PINO FARINACCI PER ANSA

FABRIZIO FERRI

GUZMAN

THIBAULT JEANSON

ROXANNE LOWIT

RICHARD MCLAREN

STEVEN MEISEL

TONINO MUCI

HELMUT NEWTON

FABIO PETTINARI

BRUNO RINALDI

MATTHEW ROLSTON

CANIO ROMANIELLO

PAOLO ROVERSI

FERDINANDO SCIANNA

MARCO SEVERINI

LANCE STAEDLER

ELLEN VON UNWERTH

SIMON WATSON

boutiques

ALBERTA FERRETTI

ITALY
Milano - Via Montenapoleone 21
Roma - Via Condotti 34
Capri - Via Camerelle 14/b

GREAT BRITAIN
London SW1 - 205/206 Sloane Street
London SW1X73J - Harvey Nichols, 109-125 Knightsbridge

UNITED STATES
New York - 452 West Broadway

JAPAN
Tokyo - 7-3, 6-Chome Minami Aoyama Minato-Ku
Osaka - Shinsai Bashi Opa B1F, 1-4-3 Nishishinsaibashi, Chuo-Ku

KOREA
Seoul 135-112 - Galleria Dept. Store, 2nd Floor, 515 Abgujeongdong, Kangnamku
Seoul 135-111 - Hyunday Dept. Store, B 2nd Floor, 429 Abgujeongdong, Kangnamku

HONG KONG
Kowloon - Shop G29, 29A G/F Hyatt Regency Hotel
Central - Shop 118-119 1/F Edinburgh Tower, The Landmark

INDONESIA
Jakarta 10230 - Plaza Indonesia Level 1, Unit 30 JI M.H. Thamrin Kav. 28-30

PHILOSOPHY by ALBERTA FERRETTI

ITALY
Milano - Via Montenapoleone 19
Roma - Via Frattina 60
Capri - Via Camerelle 29

GREAT BRITAIN
London SW1 - 205/206 Sloane Street
London SW1X73J - Harvey Nichols, 109-125 Knightsbridge

UNITED STATES
New York - 452 West Broadway
New York 10019 - Bergdorf Goodman, 754 5th Avenue

KOREA
Seoul 135-122 - Galleria Dept. Store, 3rd Floor, 515 Abgujeongdong, Kangnamku
Seoul 135-111 - Hyunday Dept. Store, B 2nd Floor, 429 Abgujeongdong, Kangnamku